REFLECT.RELEASE.
REBIRTH.

CHERAE MABRY

Cherae Mabry

About the Author

With over 80 romance books published under her nom de plume, ***Reflect. Release. Rebirth.*** is her most intimate and inspirational work of art yet. She uses her bold, and creative voice to inspire heart-led empaths to deep connection with themselves and their immediate world. She alchemizes her words into energetic currents meant to draw attention to the hidden spaces in our hearts where bold truth and love can grow. As an advocate of radical self-love, Cherae is also a certified Tantra-based love coach and yoga instructor. When she isn't lending her heart and soul to paper; she's reading, laughing and enjoy her loved ones.

Stay connected with her on Instagram **@TheCherae.**

For business opportunities or any other inquiries please email her at **cherae.mabry@gmail.com**

Foreword

Thank you for purchasing Reflect. Release. Rebirth. These poems were born out of one my most pivotal transformation cycles where I went deep within myself to unearth old patterns, thoughts, beliefs and exposed them to the light.

While reflecting on these old patterns, I took notice of which ones were getting in the way of me thriving. If there was an action holding me back from the love, career and lifestyle that I truly wanted, I did the work of releasing it.

Taking stock of my behaviors and patterns wasn't easy. In fact, I lost sleep, cried, felt pain deep down to my core and wanted to give up. But I knew that something greater was on the other side.

And I was right. A sweet rebirth occurred. Shedding the heartbreak, the bad habits and negative thoughts lead me to being closer to my truest self; a thriving queen with a heart and will to serve others.

I chose the title **REFLECT. RELEASE. REBIRTH.** because I've learned that this is the most consistent and therapeutic process of renewing yourself. At our core we are the original essence of love but living a life filled with trauma and society's expectations causes us to grow layers of muck.

To truly live the life of your dreams, it's essential to step back and REFLECT on what's working and what's not working. Then RELEASE those what's not working. And finally, go through REBIRTH, by living in a way that supports your thriving.

These poems were born out of a year of shadow work, inner child healing and pleasure practices. And it's with my highest intention that they inspire and help you heal.

May this book of poems hold you and wrap you up in love, just as writing it did for me.

Love,

Cherae Mabry

Reflect

stare into your eyes
until discomfort rises
until you want to turn away
until your reflection becomes
unbearable
unrecognizable
unconsolable
then tell yourself the truth

Glitter

---

you like some of me
not the sum of me
you like my glitter that
reflects back your light
not my dark rooms
the would develop your soul

More

I gazed up at the broad black sky
and a trail of fear blazed down my spine
Wings too vast to stay planted on the ground
but the anxiety and fear keeps me staring around
With as many options as the universe has stars
I hear God whispering become who you truly are
The only thing known in the unknown was me
and what I mistook for an empty black hole
would actually set me free

So I prepare
and I inhale
and ascend,
hoping to excel

But my feet
feel like they weigh more than my dreams
and I know that a sticky earth
is just an illusion
and that my God isn't one of confusion

But I fear drowning in the depth of the sky
Amongst the atmosphere, what lies?
And a voice tells me there is more…
More of who you already are
More of who you'll be
More than you thought you would receive

And if I want to expand
I have to trust that I'll be guided to soar
I know what I must do before I gain more

So I'll eat what's on my plate
And I'll sip what's in my cup
And I'll clear out my closet
Because space needs to be made
If I'm going to have room to be great.

What's normal anyway?

I keep trying to be normal
blend into the pattern
when I'm an anomaly
a stitch that can't be flattened

I'll unravel the fabric
swing from the threads
bold, wild and free
like in the jungle as I was born to be

Anxiety

I feel like I'm always in motion
ready to escape to the next moment
nail biting
heart racing
always ready
to hit the pavement
on the edge about to leap
a constant battle where I fight sleep
or sleep fights me
I can't wait for it to be over
or for it to never come
expectations and worries
pile up in my lungs
and I'm at war with my breath
I'm at war with my life
I'm at war with my death
I feel dragged by the future
and tethered to the past
I know that neither truly exist
And the present moment is all that I have
but it doesn't matter
when every second ticks
louder than my heart
but never detonates
just tears my mind apart
rips me from the now
always stressed about the next start

Loss Prevention

---

it's easy to lose those delicate parts
when you don't keep stock
its easy for others to run off
with your heart under their shirt
because you were looking down
looking around
at everything but your inventory
when everyone else, but you,
is keeping tabs
on what makes you whole
it's easy to lose
when you lose count

Table

you ask what does she bring to the table
when she is the table
so, what will you bring her?
A level ground to stand on?
A center piece to increase her beauty?
Nourishment to thrive?
Or will you bring so much clutter
that her top caves in and her legs wobble
weakened by your insecurity?

Mantra

too many men
have mispronounced my name
record scratching shards to my ears
but you repeat me
like the mantra I am.

Cupid 001

---

apparently not all deities need to be prayed to
some act on their own behalf
out of boredom maybe?
or just a gods need to create.

Reflect.Release. Rebirth.

Cupid 002

---

an angel or demon of a deity I'm not even sure
    I know
let alone worship
Came down and hurled me full force
in front of a stranger
I never asked to meet
but I'm now obsessed with

Legend

I heard a legend about you
that if I say your name 3 times
I'll fall in love
so, what's your nickname?
because I'm still picking thorns out
from the last time I fell

K.A.C.

I just want to be considered
on sunny days
when everything is going your way
and all your gaps are filled
but you still want me in your space

Heart-Burn

when you're angry
you become a dragon
starting a forest fire
unconfined and unforgiving
leaving me homeless

when I'm angry
I choke on my flames
suffocating on embers
hoping you don't see
my heart burn

Reflect.Release. Rebirth.

Insecure

---

you stroke my acne scarred face
and tell me I'm beautiful
I hopping you haven't lied about anything else

Shadow work 001

sometimes I pry myself open
to see what shadows are still lurking
which ones are still whispering
in my padded heart
where their voices are absorbed
a shock I can't feel
they circle in the dark
begging to be dragged to the light
by a hand that loves them

Shadow work 002

pull out the fine linens
the China and crystal too
cook the five course meal
eat in the "don't sit" dining room
dress to impress
but take off your cool
because they're never leaving
so you might as well clear out some room

400 years

you avoided the pain
and didn't toil the root
you complained of rain
but then ate the fruit
said the skin was a stain
but still drank the juice

Reflect.Release. Rebirth.

Fake Love

---

they'll destroy you
then get on their high horse
to visit your lowest valley
where they'll snap selfies at your ruins

Fire

oh you're in love
whats it feel like
… like floating on fire
while praying for more wind

Starve

---

you can't overdose on love
but without it
you will starve

life 001

from womb to dirt
there's gonna be a lot of joy
and a lot of hurt

Reflect.Release. Rebirth.

---

ocean

---

the ocean creeps to our feet to tell us secrets
let your ear hold them like a spiral sea shell

Paralyzed

not sure which is worse
over thinking
or under acting
because they both leave me paralyzed

Reflect.Release. Rebirth.

Spoken

---

your words can be oxygen
or they can be pollution
you can give life with the tongue
or you can wield confusion

Natural Laws

I could've used a heads up
to prepare for you
maybe would've picked up some new skills
like spinning straw to gold
or stopping time
perhaps breathing under water
because for you I'll break natural laws
just don't break my natural heart

Indulgence

---

loving you is like
indulging in the last bite
over and over

Delicate

we are delicate with each other
like we haven't already cracked
like we haven't chipped along the edges
like those chipped edges hasn't cut someone else
like we haven't spill ocean water on our pillows
like we haven't caused a flood on someone else's
like we haven't caved and been trapped
like we didn't have a great escape
like we haven't iced our bruised egos
like our bruised egos haven't iced us
like our hearts haven't leathered
like pulling one stitch would leave us undone
like we aren't willing to do it all over again
when we are

Tongues haiku

---

how we speak in tongues
an entire conversation
but no words uttered?

Offering

you owe those
who stretched their faith
to believe in you
more than you believe in yourself
those that have splinters
from dragging their own crosses
deserve some of your light
crack off a piece of that gold
and put in the offering

Insta-Home

my space isn't Instagramable
corners collect artifacts of impulse buys
while unfinished poems insulate my sheets
a pile of clothes may come alive
and tuck me in if I don't pay them any attention

my home isn't adorned with the latest trends
that would make you envious
but it is a reflection of my beautiful yet chaotic
    mind
it's filled with imperfections
but it's perfectly mine

Impressions

who are you trying to impress
when you're searching for the right angle?
who are you trying to impress
when you're cropping out the mess
to hide the worst, only to share the best
is their gaze truly worthy
if they can't accept your good, bad and ugly.

Where's There

There's no destination
There's no place to be
There's not even a halfway point
There's no when you get there
There's no there!
There's only the journey
So walk it
Or just sit
Let it wash over you head
Let it breeze over your shoulders
Let it whisper in passing
Let it howl and holler
Shock you
Fright you
Love you
Kiss you
Make you laugh
Make you cry
Because that's where there is.

Timeline

no matter where I am in this timeline
I will not regret a moment
for I am fully present
and can extract wisdom from every situation
the good and the bad

The Garden is You

---

whenever you don't feel seen
you don't feel beautiful
you don't feel like you belong

stand in a garden
and let the flowers
mirror you

Lover

what kind of lover are are you
do you cocoon
precisely spinning silk
to protect then hatch wings

are you mud
heavy and dark
where tongue fleshed lotuses spring

are you a willow
covering, tenderly listening
and truth whispering

Sol Mate

I'm in Love with you
And we haven't even met
but when I sleep
I feel our consciousness connect
So let our consciousness collect
On our past lives debts
As the universe rearranges worlds
I pray ours combine
So that I can be your
north, east, south and west
I will be the rhythm in your chest
your heart beat
I wanna be in your every breath
So look for me
Keep your eyes open
Cuz when we collide
We'll contribute to the divine
You my sun, I your moon
We give birth to planets,
We'll put stars to shame
We'll shine
So look for me
My eyes are open too
because you were made for me
and I for you
So lets love cuz we're overdue

Slow

love me slow enough
to fit in between wavelengths
until heartbeats sync
until skin feels as if that's all there is
until a second lasts a year
and you look up and don't know how you got here

The Swipe is Right

---

digital carousel
swipe and go round
no true connection
no love to be found
just highly curated feeds
and filtered tears of a clown
plenty of fish in the sea
but an endless search will make you drown

maybe we've taken things a little too far
when we let an algorithm manage our hearts
over indulging in options
forever raising the bar
until it's out of reach
and we don't know who we are

a swipe to the right
several to the left
dismissive in split seconds
but confused when there's nothing left

Unplug

her phone's screen is smashed
thumbs collect broken glass
every time she swipes to pay overdue bills
distracted by posts and ads
she looks at herself in the black mirror
wishing for things she's never had
for things she doesn't need
the algorithm keeps her feeling
lonely
unloved
and incomplete
so she swipes
for another hit of dopamine
her most precious senses
being exploited by
a soulless machine
an endless string of upgrades
because for an inhuman bot
her body
her mind
was never going to be enough anyway

Valuables

---

we walk around with these valuables
that can't be hidden
but they tell us
this is the only way
wear a longer skirt
hide your smile
look straight a head
don't be friendly

if you break these rules
then you've invited whatever comes to you
because men's actions
are somehow your responsibility
when we all know the truth...

Lie

people lie to themselves
on themselves
filter their faces
their voices
their lives
pretending to be a version
that only exists in virtual reality

people lie to themselves
and it's no surprise
that they'll lie to you too

Habits

they say it takes 21 days to form a new habit
well, I've known you for 42
twice the time it takes to make you apart of my
    brain wave pattern
my thoughts explode then scatter
when I'm with you
I trip over words like drunks trip over curbs
because your energy alters wave lengths
I may not make much sense
since I am unable to articulate
I am only able to say...
I am only able to say???
damn, to forget English, it took 21 days
habits
you are the first thought upon waking
this scares me because its only been 42 days
and these thoughts have become ingrained
it's too late to not have hopes
you are already a habit, that I don't care to break
smokers, nail biters, liars... they have theirs
and, well, I have you.

Cage

you cage your heart
because you know
men break in
steal things
things that cannot be replaced
your time
your passion
your energy
you keep guard
because you know you are priceless

Stairway

the stairway to your heart
may not have a banister to hold
along those steep stairs
that wobble with each step
those stairs may be
uncovered
unfinished
unleveled
and that incline punches fear in those who try
but the arrival to the top it's well worth the climb

Type

I have a type
they say
the names change
but they all fade
into updates
of the first heartbreaker

Rhythm

---

you can slide into the cracks of my broken heart
you might not be able to catch the light
But you'll be able to dance to the rhythm

Texture

I lusted for your texture
climbed your jagged mountains
admired your serrated edges
until I was sliced open
spilling all over your rough hands

Reflect.Release. Rebirth.

No means no

---

don't let the wizardry of his lies
turn your no into yes
don't let him alchemize your
boundaries into floodgates
not if you're not ready
not if it's not a yes screaming from your core

49

Excorcism

I got demons
I swear I do
They make my head spin
Make me say things that ain't true
Make me hateful, when in fact I love you
Right now all I see is black
And that ain't no excuse
Can I blame the devil
For what I did to you
Them things I said
I never gave them permission to leave my mouth
That demon I got, he let them out!
All these controlling spirits,
and you're not trying to hear it
U say I can't blame the devil
But can I blame God
I know that sounds pretty odd
But see God created Satan
And me too
Omniscient
He knew what the devil would do
Knew them demons would possess me too
See I'm a victim just like you
So pull out the holy water, your cross and a Bible
Call a priest
We gon' fix this tonight
Cuz baby I ain't lie!

I ain't no deceiver
But please be a believer
The angels sing BELIEVE HER
Don't just watch my head spin
Please do something!
I need an intervention!
I know, I'm no Christian but can we please try an
    Exorcism??

Heavy

his words were air
I floated intoxicated for a while
but the crash was inevitable
because a mouth that blows lies
cannot hold you
for the truth is solid
and my heart is made of gold

Phoenix

---

his tongue set fire
to a place you loved
a place between the gaps in your heart
though gone up in smoke
you will rise from the ashes
of the bridge he burned

Self Sabotage

I get in my own way
block my own view
shackle my self to outdated beliefs
that keep me from jumping
into the unknown and vast
ocean of my success

Battles

I pick my battles
like fruit from a tree
I won't touch it
if it won't nourish me

Sunlight

sun light rips through blinds
and weeps on your eyes
the unease of day burns your face
and you don't know what to expect
but you gotta get up anyway

Nudes

---

you ask for nudes
so I undress my tongue for you
I got a body of words to bare
that don't blush under your stare
you can take it or leave it
you can love it or hate it
since my truth wasn't expected
when you asked to see me naked

Mindless

I've considered losing my mind
one cell at a time
rounding up my fucks
and shooting them one by one
down the line

Unravel

---

last time you fell in love
you busted your heart wide open
only to later stuff
& stitch it with memories
that you keep unraveling

Down

I get down
don't bury yourself with me
just leave lilies on my dirt

Behind

you left things behind
that I cannot burn
pawn
giveaway
throw out on the lawn to be stolen
the things you left
are worn on my shoulders
heavy in my chest
anchoring me
to the center of an unmade bed

Addiction

when the things you want
turn into needs
they spawn addiction

when the things you're addicted to
don't need you
they spawn death

Babel

---

the love that dropped you to your knees
without anyone to bow your head to
because you were robbed of your God
& now your faith can't conjoin your palms
so you sit there speaking in tongues
languages you don't even understand.

Rose

everybody wants to hold a rose
until their pricked
but you can take a thorn to your side
never to your back
and I won't test your pain tolerance
just don't pull my petals

Daddy Issues 001

---

we are the flowers
our fathers were too empty to water
but we grow and flourish anyway

Dramatic escape

I let my pain rest with the stars
while I was cradled by the moon
because in the dark no one can see my tears
and if they do, I can just say it's raining

Wine at Dawn

you make me drink wine at dawn
so I can get some sleep
right when the sun comes to peak
and the birds start to sing
you make me want to miss all of that beauty
just so that I can drink you into a faded memory

Empty

you keep filling your body with bodies
when it's your soul that's empty
you think you can patch up that hole in your heart
with another person's parts
when no one will ever be able to fulfill you
because they're all empty too

68

Sunbathe

I bathed in the sun
to wash away the darkness you left.
the shadowy stain on my heart
couldn't withstand the light of love

Pedestal

I shouldn't have placed you on that pedestal
because you came crashing down
and now I'm paralyzed under your dead weight

Lava

---

careful of those men
that leave you hot & bothered
puddled in lava
keep an eye on the ones that make the temple
between your thighs melt
they feel like heaven
but can drag you to hell

side effects

you want to get to know me
say I intrigue you
my smile makes you comfortable
that I'm a chaise lounge
where you can spill the secrets
you thought you had to die with
secrets you were prepared to feed the worms
so you tell me things I didn't want to know
you want the same in return
want me to smash open my heart
and be reciprocal
But I'm stubborn
I don't crack as easy
I've been sealed with gold
a knowledge that if I let go
I can't come back
so you put in the work
all the effort
and peel back layers
you're shocked I stain your fingers
and that I get under your skin
you weren't prepared for this reaction
that no cure
no herbs
no drugs can manage
your heart beats different now
and you can't unsee me dancing to the beat

Barbed Wire

---

his lies wrap around your raw heart
like barbed wire
it beats for him
then bleeds for him
how will you pry it free?

Free Heart

the parts of you that you tucked away
from the light
out of fear that you'd be left out of the tribe
they burn your stomach
ache your head
and keep you up at night
those parts that you hide from the world
will break your heart trying to get free

No reverse

you may not be able to rewind
but you can always change your mind

Silent Stars

I stayed up past everyone's bed time
waiting for a hint of peace
a hint of light
and all I found was silence
from the stars
and the cracking of my heart

...end

---

in the end
we have no choice
but to be down to earth

Dawn

dawn cracks
and floods us
with the light of possibility
yet we hit snooze
and bemoan yesterday
as if it were the present

Breathe

the universe has a way of vacuuming space
I didn't realize was cluttered
but my God can I breathe easier

Mourning

Some mornings the sun has to beg
for us to get out of bed
and He pulls on the eyes blinded closed
as our heads lay heavy and dents pillows
while we beg in our dreams for more comfort
that won't come

those mornings feel more like curses than blessings
more like hell, than heaven
and even if they dare to come back
they all eventually fade into black

Submerge

I filled the tub
with hot water
to steam out the muck of the day
to melt my worries
and keep them at bay

I salted the water
like I would a stew
hoping that it would draw out
the essence of you

when I sank in
I drowned all my sins
I saw where you end
and I could where I begin

then I emerged
still feeling quite blue
it's going to more than a bath
maybe a baptism
to get over you

Worthy

Always desired
never deserved
always giving
rarely served
never been fed
but always dessert
when will you ever
fully learn your worth?

Smile

if it doesn't make me smile
until my cheeks ache
and makes me forget my last heartbreak
it's not the love for me
it sounds like misery

Shells & Seeds

We shared sunflower seeds
sitting on the porch above concrete
ditch the shells
to get to the center
to the best part
right to the heart
he holds a special place
we were best friends
he was a soulmate
now I don't love him like
your mother loves your father,
like you loved your ex,
like you'll love your next
but I love him
in a different way
not quite under the sun
but over the moon
we would spend the entire month of June
hiding and seeking
we would play tag
and I wanted to be it
So in the open I hid
hoping he would find me
but he never did
we just weren't compatible
when we truth or dared kissed I felt we were judged
    by shadows

we would chase ice cream trucks
search for 4 leaf clovers for luck
until the summer he left me
I felt so stuck
But he was worse off
without each other we were both lost
life stretched us
in different directions
but some how we found our way back
I knew things had changed
time had suffocated our innocence
we were not the same
he came back around
we were reintroduced
and when he returned
I asked him what did he learn
he said his dreams had been lynched off of
    basketball hoops
and he wasn't sure of who he was nor his roots
now he picks seeds out his weed
I collect shells off the beach
we sit close but still out of reach
we try to relate to one another
as we reminisce with each other
sitting on the porch above concrete
sharing sunflower seeds

Empty

hHe left a pulsing hole
and you try to fill it
with friends
food
shopping
a new "he"
but the pulsing hole is a sore
that doesn't need to be filled
it just needs to breathe

Misery

if misery loves company
give me solitary confinement
I'd rather be alone in the silence
with nothing but the thrum of my heartbeat
than crowded with demons and screams of toxicity

Contortion

you will never be perfect
no matter how many times you fold yourself
you won't fit into that box
your limbs will stick out of the sides
waving to be seen
hands hoping to be held
your voice will bounce off of walls
and seep out the cracks
finding any ear willing to listen
because your essence can't be contained
you will never be perfect
because the messy edges is what makes you unique
and stuffing yourself into small places causes
    nothing but pain

Tongue Tied

because he can't take the lashings of truth
he wants you to tie your tongue into a knot
so that you go silent
while he folds your legs like origami
and plunges into the center of your earth
as if thats all you were born for.

Ugly Cry

I'm going to lay down in my bed
and pull the covers over my head
I'm going to let it rain
flush it all down the drain
I'm going to cry 'til it hurts
Hurt 'til I'm numb
and then breathe into hollow spaces
and become undone
I'll sleep in the void
until I rise with the morning joy

Pain

I can eliminate the evidence
piece by piece
scratch the essence of you off my skin
until I bleed
indulge in wine induced amnesia
to get reprieve
factory reset my phone
sprain thumbs to delete
yell I don't care until I can't breathe
I'm willing to hurt myself
to get you to leave

sometimes...

sometimes a lotus
sometimes a Venus fly trap
sometimes a lake
sometimes a tidal wave
sometimes a breeze
sometimes a storm
sometimes the cleanse
sometimes the filth
sometimes the dark room
sometimes the light at the end of the tunnel
she could heal you
or kill you
either way she's your reflection

Reflect.Release. Rebirth.

Map Quest

Head down Uncertain lane
you'll pass a screaming woman
calling you names
ignore her
her voice resembles yours
but its weak
she may trail you for a while
but don't bother to speak

just keep going like you have some place to be

the sun may set
but it always rejoins the sky
meditate when you need to
open your third eye

After a while you'll stumble upon dark and scary
    woods
you'll want to go back
but I don't think you should
stay on the path
and keep up the walk
because I guarantee you that there's gold in the
    tree's bark

when you make it through the forest
you're going to be confused

but keep on going
you have nothing to lose

you'll wonder which way to go
just listen to your heart
and go with the flow

peaks and valleys are sure to follow
but eventually you'll arrive
to the heartland that you can call home

Warmth

I wear you well
warm, like a tan
bringing out the best in me
while highlighting my gold

Bones

to return to sender
plant them
stack them
align them
upright to the red sun
so that they can burn back to dust
from where they grew from

Reflect.Release. Rebirth.

Baptise haiku

---

going with the flow
you'll be baptized in honey
but will never drown

Anger 001

don't fear the fire
that's just the suns energy
burning inside of you

Reflect.Release. Rebirth.

Reciprocate haiku

---

you can love others
better by forgiving and
loving yourself first

Clarity haiku

---

you will gain the world
seeing things for what they are
don't turn a blind eye

Temple

your body isn't a fire escape
for him to flee his painful reality
your body isn't a cave
for him to hide from his demons
your body isn't a revolving door
for him to come and go leaving nothing but hot air
your body is a divine portal
that he has to be worthy to enter
your body is an alter
deserving of sacrifices and offerings

Princesses

There are some who play dead waiting for a kiss to
revive them

There are some who hide amongst their seven
shadows hoping no one finds them

There are some who burden themselves with
everyone else's mess, ignoring their power

There are some who's skin is so soft she can feel
even a pea-sized lie through flattery

Yet here we all are hiding our crowns waiting for
magic that's already in our hearts

Gold

Strong women still crack and bleed
but we heal back together
stitched with gold thread

Spring 001

it's spring
but remnants of winter remain
lifeless and cold
evidence that for a sweet rebirth
something must die

Body 001

Your body is not a mistake
Your body is not an accident
Your body doesn't need to apologize
Your body doesn't have to fit...
into societies expectations
tiny clothes
nor into his bed

Rise and Grind

if everything has its own space
and its own moment of time
then I accept the rain
to appreciate the shine
and i'll aways remember theres
no glow without the grind

S.O.S.

There's no one coming to save you
those angel wings that you're waiting to wrap
     you up
and carry you along
are already encoded down your spine
So get up!
Walk on water
because there is no rescue team
your fear is the anchor
and at any time
you can unleash it
while you're waiting for the life raft to float by
the catch of the day
is swimming away
so don't be afraid
you are the movement you've been waiting for
so push through those waves

Before Dawn

if she tilled soil before dawn
she's not interested in your excuses
for she's grown fruit in the dark
and knows fertilizer from bullshit

Forward

I watched your shadow mock you
as you marched towards the sun
each unfair critique
itching your ears
but never rooting in your mind
because you know the royalty you're
carrying in your heart
and you know that your shadow is
behind you
right where it belongs

Portal

you expect access to my body
without going through the heart
but I'm a multi-verse of portals
with a super nova in my chest
so you must walk through the fire
if you ever expect to meet the wet

Worth the Wait

even if he cannot see
you are worth the wait
worth the effort
worth the energy
it's not your fault that he is blind
and cannot see your light
but continue to shine bright

Break up

it's not a break-up
it's a breakthrough
I'm diving into myself
after falling for you
we may be ending
but I'm starting anew

My truth

yYou said I had something on my lip
and shunned it
and swiped at it
and picked at it
but it was no use
because what you saw was my truth

Honey Baby

for your benefit
for the world at large
keep me honeyed, baby
keep me soft

Pray

---

may the life you live
in between the prayers
give you less to worry God about
and more to thank Her for

Dirt

you smell like you've been outside
of your comfort zone
and your fingers taste like the dirt
from the red earth you plucked me out of

Art Embodied

If I can't be a singer
let me be the song
if can't be a poet
let me be the poem
and you can write me
recite me
sing me lightly
because
whats dripped sweeter from your tongue than
     my name
what would you trade for honey stained lips?

Plate

Fix your plate first
Pile it with the good things
The protein
The dark greens
Make sure you're satisfied
Full on life
That your belly's stuffed with wonder
Depend on no one to fulfill your hunger

Reflect.Release. Rebirth.

Infinite Soul

---

society wants us to fit into
tight spaces
tucked away
when we are stars
and space is infinite

Choke

parts of myself
are remembering they belong together
after years of breaking down into digestible bites
I no longer care if others choke on my presence

Original

That woman in your mirror
the one you criticize every time you look at her
the one you imagine another's
nose
eyes
lips
taking over her face

Please learn to
accept her
treasure her
love her
leave her voice unfiltered

because being original is priceless
so understand your full worth

Overstayed

that pain that gave you insomnia
that no tea could soothe
the one that ached no matter
what relief you pursued
the one you swore
was a permanent tattoo
the pain you pray away
will learn it's welcome is overstayed
the one that will slowly began to fade
like the moon in the brightness of day

Warm

the woman you were
before they broke your heart
is still there
keeping your love warm
ready to be served right back to you

Old Money

I inherited gold
that can't be spent
that can't be melted
down into adornments
not the kind that restrains
fingers and wrists
you can't see it
but it can't be missed

I inherited gold
that steels the tip of my tongue
that lines the inside of my heart
that exhales through my lungs

I inherited gold
that has the pull of the moon
that wafts in the air
even when I've left the room

Reflect.Release. Rebirth.

6th Sense

I don't see dead people
my selfies aren't a seance
though my smile can resurrect
the deadest of hearts
I didn't lure you from
your self imposed grave
where you should've stayed
see, when you went cold
for you I went numb
and I have many talents
but seeing ghosts ain't one

Morning Light

---

the nights that you crack open
in a flood of tears
are the nights you water your hopes
that will bloom in the morning light

Reflect. Release. Rebirth.

Who were you?

Who were you before it rained?
Who were you before the pain?

Everybody gets caught under a cloud
Some of us get watered down
And some of us drown

Who were you before the storm?
Who were you when you were born?

Chaos

I'm a mess
a spilled glass of wine
on a white carpet
a permanent stain
an imperfect shape
a state of chaos
where everything returns
and everything is made

Love Bomb

Love bomb yourself
let the sweet chaos
of your self obsession
engulf you in a sea of passionate flames
the blaze of your self love
sheds light on how others should treat you

A time...

there's a time to scorch the earth
and a time to water the garden
not knowing the difference
is how you destroy your world

Reflect.Release. Rebirth.

Away

he says
you're the one that got away
when it was his hands
that burned a bridge
that now he can't cross
to get away to you

Wounds

you may not be responsible for your wound
but you can choose to pour light through it

Brain Cells

---

locked within the cells of our minds
spells incant around wrists in a bind
unconsciously
we cast them down our spines

we rattle against cages
bouncing off open ceilings and bars
into one another
forgetting who we are

with our eyes in rest mode
we don't interrupt to see
because the day that we do
we'd finally get free

North Star

Baby girl you are enough
you're the whole ocean wrapped in flesh
with a north star for a heart
follow it's light
and know you're always close to home
with a genie lamp in your lap
every wish made comes true
when you know it all begins and ends with you

Abandon

I won't abandon my tongue
for a shallow ear
that can't hold the depths of my truth

I won't abandon my heart
for hollow hugs
that can't hold the fire of my love

And I won't abandon my soul
for shaky hands
that can't hold my light

Brilliance

I won't hide my brilliance
for fear of blinding other people
their vision is not my responsibility
but blazing through the sky is mine

Beauty Regimens

flowers aren't searching on Youtube
for a 12 step beauty regimen
they know that true beauty
comes from standing in the light.

Fall Apart

It's okay to fall apart
to crumble into dust
so that the wind can carry you
without resistance

It's okay to fall apart
and crash to the ground
so that you can be planted
to grow with persistence

It's okay to fall apart
and drop to your knees
to find strength
before standing with confidence

Reflect.Release. Rebirth.

Nothing missing

---

even if all the pieces can't be seen
you are whole
you are complete

Reflect.Release. Rebirth.

Nothing missing

---

even if all the pieces can't be seen
you are whole
you are complete

Blocked

they can mute your voice
and leave you on read
shadow ban your message
you'll still be in their head
because a vibe can't be blocked
so keep speaking the truth
and don't you ever stop

Interview

Who taught you to whisper
when your voice should be bouncing off walls?

Who taught you to tiptoe
when you should be marching through halls?

What good does it do the world to hide your face?
Who can you serve if you don't take up space?

What would it take for you to come out?
What is at stake for you to live out loud?

Myth

Being alone doesn't scare me
Being alone with someone who's mask is fused to
    the bone
horrifies me
if you can can't be real with yourself
how can you be real with anyone else
and if you can't be real
what are you
but a myth that breathes
and never lives

Reflect. Release. Rebirth.

Origins

Not the crystals
Not the water
Not the herbals
Not the Bible
Not the Tarot
Not the bones
Not the Preacher
Not the Phone
Not the sky
on your knees
where you beg and you plead
or the pool where you dip
nor meditate Bodhi tree
Not the palms
Not the prophet
Not the psalms
altar in a closet
It's been you from the start
from the dirt and to the stars

Bye Now

By now I thought I'd b enclosed in a white picket fence
    with a husband, a dog, and 2.5 kids

By now I thought I would've sailed the seven seas
    and seen all the sights from Botswana to Italy

By now I thought my account would be full of commas
    student loans would be paid and I could retire my
momma

By now I thought I would've killed my anxiety
    that depression would be gone and I'd have no worries

By now I thought I would've arrived
    but it's all a journey I realized

Bye now, so that I can go own it
    live, love, heal and savor the moment

Afterword

Dear reader,

Thank you so much for reading this poetry book. I hope that you found love, peace and strength in my words. Please connect with me on Instagram @TheCherae to stay informed on updates about new books and workshops.

If this book touched you and you found the poems resonant with your heart, please share with loved ones and leave a review.

Sending you love and healing,
Cherae Mabry